THE NEW CREEPY CRAWLY COLLECTION

ANTS

For a free color catalog describing Gareth Stevens' list of high-quality books and multimedia programs, call 1-800-542-2595 (USA) or 1-800-461-9120 (Canada). Gareth Stevens Publishing's Fax: (414) 225-0377.
See our catalog, too, on the World Wide Web: http://gsinc.com

Library of Congress Cataloging-in-Publication Data

Vaughan, Jenny.
    Ants / by Jenny Vaughan ; illustrated by Tony Gibbons.
      p. cm. -- (The New creepy crawly collection)
    Includes bibliographical references and index.
    Summary: Examines the anatomy, behavior, and colony life of ants,
as well as unusual facts about them and their nests.
    ISBN 0-8368-1910-1 (lib. bdg.)
    1. Ants--Juvenile literature. [1. Ants.] I. Gibbons, Tony, ill. II. Title. III. Series.
QL568.F7V38 1997
595.79'6--dc21   97-7344

This North American edition first published in 1997 by
Gareth Stevens Publishing
1555 North RiverCenter Drive, Suite 201
Milwaukee, Wisconsin 53212 USA

This U.S. edition © 1997 by Gareth Stevens, Inc. Created with original © 1996
by Quartz Editorial Services, 112 Station Road, Edgware HA8 7AQ U.K.

Consultant: Matthew Robertson, Senior Keeper, Bristol Zoo, Bristol, England.

Printed in Mexico

1 2 3 4 5 6 7 8 9 01 00 99 98 97

THE NEW
CREEPY CRAWLY
COLLECTION

ANTS

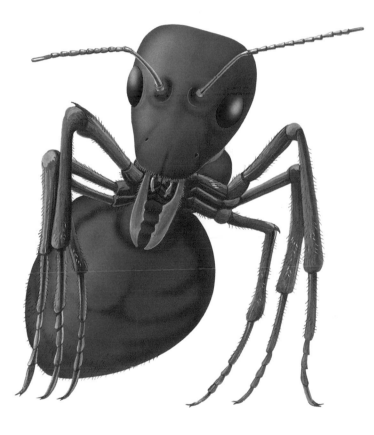

by Jenny Vaughan
Illustrated by Tony Gibbons

Gareth Stevens Publishing
MILWAUKEE

Contents

5   Getting to know ants

6   Small but strong

8   Small bugs, giant family

10 Now you see them, now you don't

12 What a team!

14 Terrible termites

16 Work, work, work!

18 Life in the colony

20 Killer armies

22 Did you know?

24 Glossary
    Books and Videos
    Index

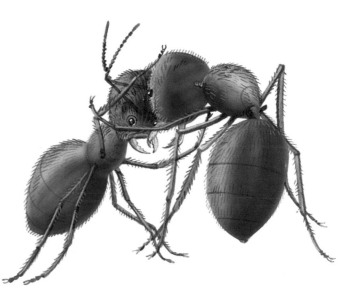

Getting to know
ants

How many different kinds of ants have you seen? You have probably spotted black ones and reddish-brown ones. You may also have seen yellow ones, and even ants that fly. But, in fact, there are thousands of different types of ants!

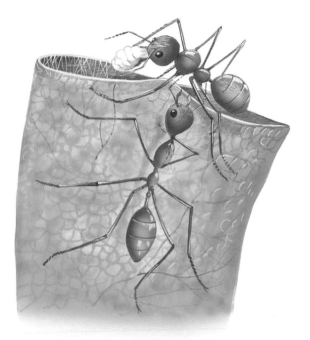

All ants are insects with six legs. Some are only about 0.08 inches (2 millimeters) long. Others are giants in comparison at about 1.2 inches (30 mm) long, close to the length of your little finger.

Ants can be found on almost every area of land in the world, except for the frozen Arctic and Antarctic. Some are mainly plant-eaters, but others feed on the flesh of dead animals. They may even hunt and kill for their food.

All ants have one thing in common: they live in colonies, or groups. Turn the pages that follow to find out all about the secret life of ants.

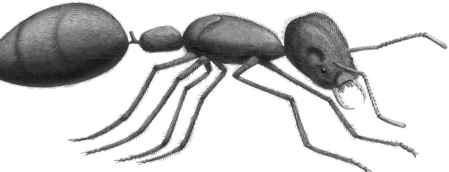

Small but

Next time you get an opportunity to take a close look at an ant, try to imagine how frightening it must seem to other small insects it might attack. As you can see in this much-larger-than-life illustration, the ant has a big head for its body size. Notice, too, the two stalks growing from it. These are its antennae, and they are used for touching, feeling, smelling, and tasting. Ants have no ears like yours, but can "hear" by detecting vibrations in the ground. Like other insects, ants have compound eyes, with up to one thousand lenses in each, instead of just one lens as humans have. Compound eyes are good for spotting movement but can only see objects that are very close.

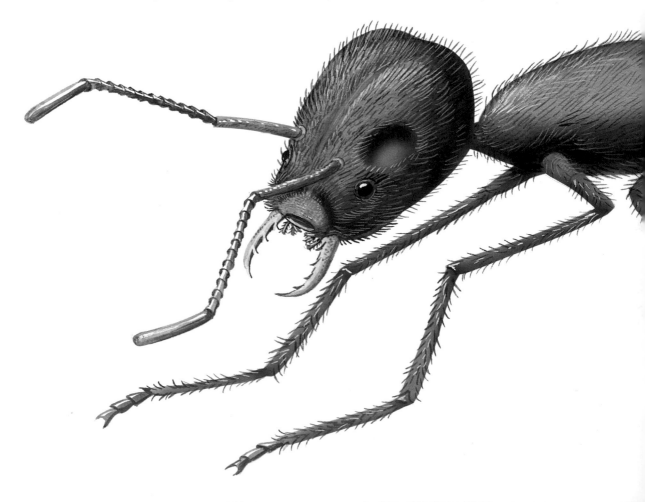

strong

The thorax is located behind the ant's head. It contains the heart as well as a passage that carries food from the head to the abdomen. The thorax also contains strong muscles, some of which power the ant's legs, which are attached to the thorax. A thin waist joins the thorax to the abdomen, where food is digested.

Some ants also have a poisonous stinger at the end of the abdomen to defend themselves against enemies. The ant's body is covered with a shell-like skin known as the exoskeleton. This protects the ant's internal organs. All male ants have wings, as do the queens. However, other types of ants, known as workers, do not have wings.

Small bugs,

There are over ten thousand different types of ants — so only a few are shown here. Black garden ants are a very common type. They live in meadows, forests, and gardens. You may have seen them crawling around, as in the drawing *below*.

If you have ever come across flying ants, they were probably black garden ants, *above*. The males and queens have wings. Soon after they become adults, all the males and queens leave the nest where they were born and fly into the air in a process called swarming. All the males die soon after mating with the queen.

giant family

South American leaf-cutter ants, such as the one shown *below*, grow fungus in their nests as a food supply. First, the ants cut pieces from leaves. Back in the nest, they chew and then spread the leaves around the fungus, as compost.

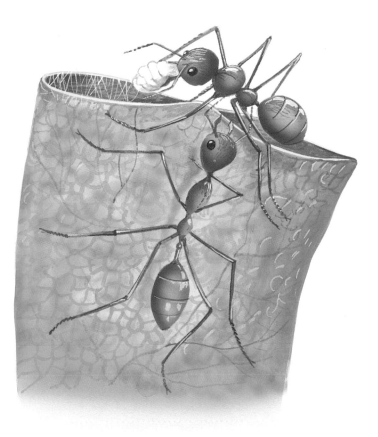

Tailor ants, like those from India, *above*, are also known as weaver ants. These ants make their nests from leaves. They move their larvae back and forth between leaves in a tree. The larvae then spin sticky silk, which holds the leaves together to form a nest.

Now you see them,

Imagine you are standing in a woods or a meadow. You might see many different kinds of birds and insects. But you will probably not spot ants unless you look very closely.

A small wooded area can be home to millions of ants. The reason you cannot see them is that they are so small and dark. This dark color acts as camouflage — that is, coloring that makes the ants hard to see against their surroundings.

Many ants live in the soil or underground most of the time. This makes them harder to spot because they are black or brown.

now you don't

European wood ants live mostly in pine woods. They are reddish brown, which makes them hard to see among dead leaves. They pile pine needles and sticks over their nests, so that the nests, too, are often hard to spot.

Some kinds of carpenter ants, which live in dead wood, are brown — a good color for an insect that needs to hide in the dark bark of trees.

Other ants, such as yellow meadow ants, live in grassy places. Their bodies merge well with the dead, sun-baked grasses that lie on the meadow floors. They, too, are well camouflaged in their environment.

11

What a

Anyone who sees an ant nest immediately notices how busy all the ants are. Most of the ants in a nest are workers. These are all females. They look after the queen, or queens, which lay all the eggs. The workers also care for the larvae that hatch from the eggs.

After a while, the larvae spin cocoons for themselves and become pupae. At this point, they begin to turn into adult ants. The workers care for these, too.

One of the workers' most important tasks is to collect food for the entire colony of ants. Larger workers, sometimes called soldiers, have another role. They must defend the colony. If the colony is disturbed, all the workers try to save the young. The soldiers will attack, using their jaws and their stingers, if necessary.

team!

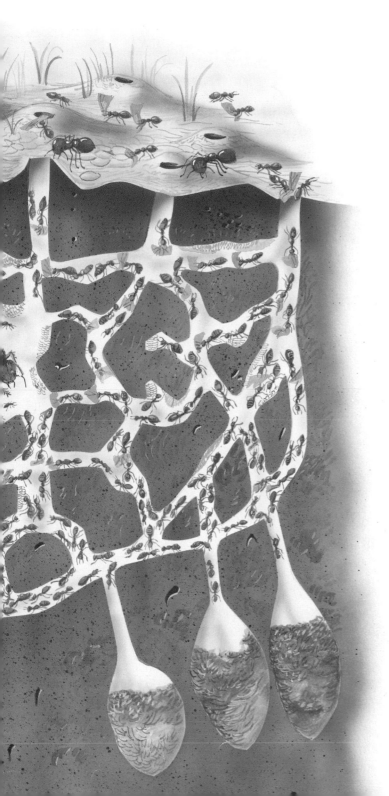

Along with the queen and the workers, there are also males and young queens in the nest. These ants have wings, and they fly away soon after emerging from their cocoons. The males' only job is to mate with the queens, which can then lay their own eggs and start a new colony.

An ant nest cannot survive unless all the ants work well together and communicate. They do this by means of smell. Each nest has its own scent. This helps the ants recognize each other. Ants also use scent trails to guide each other to good sources of food.

The nest shown here belongs to a colony of leaf-cutter ants. Look carefully and see if you can spot the queen, her eggs, the workers, and the soldiers.

Terrible termites

Termites are light-colored insects from tropical parts of the world, such as Africa and South America. They live in a manner so similar to ants that they are sometimes called "white ants." But, in fact, they are not closely related to ants.

Termites look very different from ants, too — their bodies are softer and paler than ants' bodies, and they do not have a narrow waist.

Most termites usually live underground. They may grow fungi, as some ants do, or collect grain, as harvester ants do, for food. They also eat dead wood, which ants rarely do. Some termites build tall nests, called termite mounds, using soil, wood, and their own droppings and saliva.

Some of these nests have amazing shapes, like the one you can see here, and some may even reach a height of over 20 feet (6 meters).

Termites are often considered pests because of the terrible damage they can do to wooden buildings by eating away at them.

Like an ant nest, a termite colony starts with a male and a queen mating in a swarm. But unlike ants, the male — or king — termite does not die. Instead, it stays with the queen in the nest.

The queen lays up to three thousand eggs a day, and the termites may live up to twenty years. Worker termites look after the nest, and soldiers defend it, as with ants. The worker and soldier termites are females, but they never fly and do not normally lay eggs, as the queens do.

Termite young are known as nymphs. When they hatch from their eggs, they already look like adult termites. Interestingly, the closest relative to a termite is the cockroach!

Work, work,

People have always been fascinated by how hard ants seem to work. In the Book of Proverbs in the Old Testament of the Bible, there is some good advice dating from thousands of years ago that uses the ant as an example: "Go to the ant, thou sluggard. Consider her ways and be wise." (*Sluggard* means "lazy person.") The story explains how, in summer, ants go out and collect food and store it for the winter. In other words, we should work hard and prepare for our future needs.

In the same way, a writer from Ancient Greece named Aesop wrote a fable (a story with a lesson) about ants that used a similar idea.

The fable tells of a grasshopper that did nothing but sing all summer, while the ants worked hard to collect and store grain for the winter. The grasshopper laughed at the ants for working so hard while she lazed around.

When winter came, the grasshopper had nothing to eat. She begged the ants for food.

"What were you doing all summer, while we were working?" asked the ants. "Singing," said the grasshopper. And the ants refused to help her.

work!

Life in

An ant colony usually begins with a single queen. After she has mated with a male, the queen makes a small chamber for herself in the soil and lays her eggs. She bites off her wings, since they get in the way underground.

Ants are certainly brilliant architects and builders!

Many ants make large nests, often with several chambers and linking passages. After making her first chamber, the queen does not work any more. It is the worker ants that continue to dig out new chambers and passages.

Nests can vary enormously in their form. They are built underground, under stones or logs, or sometimes even hanging from trees.

Once the larvae hatch, the queen feeds them with her saliva. This is the only time the queen has to care for herself and others without help.

the colony

The young ants now develop into workers that, from then on, look after the nest.

The workers also gather food for themselves, the young, and the queen. If, by chance, the larvae are not getting enough warmth and moisture, the workers will even move the larvae to another chamber. The workers are always very busy.

Ants are immensely strong for their size. As they dig tunnels, they may carry stones or leaves that weigh many times more than they do.

Just imagine how strong you would have to be to carry something perhaps fifty times as heavy as you are!

Killer

It is dawn in a South American forest, and something is moving on the ground under the trees. A large colony of stinging army ants is on the march.

These ants spend much of their lives marching by day and resting at night, clustered around their queen, eggs, and larvae. Now, as the morning light reaches the forest floor, they begin to form a column about 10 feet (3 m) wide. The leading ants set off, leaving a trail of scent. The others follow.

Soldier ants march on the outside of the column for defense. The queen and other workers march in the center, carrying the eggs and larvae.

armies

Scouts break away from the column to look for food. One group fans out and swarms quickly over its prey, a large moth, stinging and smothering it to death. Others divide into smaller columns and attack anything in their way.

The forest fills with low-pitched sound as leaves rustle and other small insects buzz in warning about this killer army.

Army ants march every day while the young are still larvae. When the young reach the stage of becoming pupae (prior to full adulthood), however, the ants need less food. The killer army will settle in one area for a while before marching again.

Did you know?

What do ants eat?
Ants eat many forms of food, including seeds, flower nectar, other insects, fungi, and honeydew. The ants usually get honeydew from aphids.

Which ants can sting?
Many ants that sting belong to a group that includes a common type of red ant. Driver ants from Africa and the army ants of South America also sting. Some ants do not sting but can squirt poison from their abdomens. Other ants are harmless.

Which ants can fly?
The only ants that can fly are the males and the young queens, when they leave the nest.

Do other animals live in ant nests?
Animals that may share ant nests include aphids (which provide honeydew), mites, certain types of beetles (which the ants may even feed), the caterpillar of the large blue butterfly, and a kind of white woodlouse.

▼ What are the main enemies of ants?
Birds are ants' main enemies. The African aardvark also enjoys a meal of ants, as does the South American anteater, which catches ants (and termites) by poking its long, sticky tongue into their nests. The echidna, known as the "spiny anteater," is an Australian mammal that eats ants, too.

▶ *Do ants fight?*
Worker ants sometimes fight members of other colonies of the same species. Some have fierce battles, and many are killed before the winners take over the enemy nest. Other kinds, such as honey-pot ants, just push each other around — but the winners still take over the nest.

Are ants useful?
Some ants help control other insects that may be pests. Certain wood ants are protected by law in some places because of this.

How do ants reproduce?
Usually, only the queen ant lays eggs. She mates with a male just once after she leaves the nest where she hatched. She never mates again.

How fast can most ants move?
A scientist recently calculated that the army ant, which is 0.4 inches (1 centimeter) long, can move along at 10 feet (3 m) per minute —that's 0.11 miles (0.18 kilometers) per hour. This may sound slow. But think of the size of a small family car. This car is about 450 times longer than an ant. Now multiply the ant's speed by 450, and you'll see that the ant's rate is the equivalent of around 50 miles (81 km) per hour. That's not as fast as a car can go at top speed, but it is still impressive and a lot faster than *you* can run! Some ants move even faster than this over short distances. Scientists estimate, for example, that one type of desert ant from Africa can run at the equivalent of 100 miles (160 km) per hour!

23

Glossary

abdomen — one of the three main body parts of an insect. An ant's abdomen is located behind the thorax and contains the stomach.

antennae — thin, movable sense organs on an insect's head that are used for smelling, feeling, and tasting.

aphids — tiny, soft-bodied insects, also known as plant lice, that suck juice from plants.

cocoon — a silk casing that an ant pupa spins around itself and in which it develops into an adult.

exoskeleton — a hard, outside body covering.

fungus (plural *fungi*) — plants without flowers, leaves, or green coloring. Mushrooms, toadstools, and some molds are *fungi*.

larva (plural *larvae*) — a wingless, wormlike insect that is newly hatched.

nectar — a sweet liquid found in many flowers. Nectar is a good food source for insects.

nymph — a young insect that has a shape similar to the adult form.

pupa (plural *pupae*) — the stage of an insect's growth when it is developing into an adult inside a cocoon.

thorax — the middle part of an insect's body. The ant's thorax contains the heart.

Books and Videos

Ant. Kitty Benedict (Creative Education)

Ant. David Hawcock (Random Books for Young Readers)

Ants: A Great Community. Secrets of the Animal World series. (Gareth Stevens)

The Ant. (Barr Films)

Ant Life. (International Film Bureau)

Insects in a Garden. (Encyclopædia Britannica Educational Corporation video)

Index

anteaters 22
ants: colonies of 5, 12, 13, 18-19, 20, 23; and communication 13; eating habits of 5, 9, 21, 22; enemies of 22; habitat of 5, 8, 10-11; mating and reproduction of 8, 12, 13, 18, 23; nests of 8, 9, 11, 12, 13, 18, 22, 23; physical characteristics of 5, 6-7; types of 5, 7, 8, 10, 11, 12; wings of 7, 8, 13, 18

army ants 20-21, 22, 23

black garden ants 8

camouflage 10, 11
carpenter ants 11

desert ants 23
driver ants 22

harvester ants 14
honey-pot ants 23

larvae (ant) 9, 12, 18, 19, 20, 21

leaf-cutter ants 9, 13

queen ants 7, 8, 12, 13, 18, 19, 20, 22, 23

red ants 22

scent trails 13, 20
soldier ants 12, 13, 20

tailor ants 9

wood ants 11, 23
worker ants 7, 12, 13, 18, 19, 23

yellow meadow ants 11

24